Light Night

Written by Teresa Heapy

Illustrated by Claire Keay

Collins

I get a bit sad in the winter.
The darkness and gloom
seem to spoil things.

It's hard to do the sports I like.

"Can I go and shoot hoops with Craig in the park?" I said.

"No, Fred," sighed my dad.

"In the winter, the park shuts at dusk."

"It's too dark out there," my mum pointed out.

"That's not the slightest bit fair!" I groaned.

"Winter can be fun," said my dad.
"We can swoosh torches to get patterns.
We can drink hot, sweet milk."

I still felt glum.

Then today, my mum said, "Grab a scarf! Let's go out!"

"But it's dark!" I said.

"There is a Light Night fair just down the street," she said. "Come on!"

So we went out in the dark.

The park was glimmering with bright, sparkling lights! There were lights like stars in the trees.

There were swings and speeding bumper cars. We got sweet toffee and hot drinks.

Then a rocket swooshed up high.
There was a faint flicker of light, then
a boom!

Silver shimmers of light were sweeping and twisting in the dark. "Fantastic!" I said. It was thrilling.

My mum and dad held me tight.
I felt my gloom lifting.

"Let's come back to Light Night next year!" I said. "Perhaps winter is not so bad."

Fred and the Light Night fair

🐾 Review: After reading 🐾

Use your assessment from hearing the children read to choose any GPCs, words or tricky words that need additional practice.

Read 1: Decoding

- Discuss the meaning of the following vocabulary in context:
  - Page 4: **pointed out** Ask: Does this mean "mentioned" or did Fred's mum point with her finger? (*"mentioned" because* **pointed** *comes after the words she said*)
  - Page 5: **swoosh** Ask: Is this describing the type of torches or what Fred's dad said they can do with them? (*what they can do with them – they can move them fast through the air to get patterns*)
- Turn to the following pages and challenge the children to sound out the words with adjacent consonants and long vowels.

Page 8: **glimmering   bright   sparkling   stars   trees**   Page 9: **speeding   sweet**

- Challenge the children to read pages 8 and 9 fluently. Say: Can you blend in your head when you read the words?

Read 2: Prosody

- Turn to pages 10 and 11, and discuss how **swooshed** and **boom** are like the noise/movement they are describing.
- Challenge the children to read page 10 with expression, emphasising and lengthening these words to sound like the fireworks.
- Repeat for page 11, pointing out the words **shimmers, sweeping, twisting**. Discuss which of these words might be lengthened when they read the page (e.g. **sweeping** *to reflect the long sweeping motion*).

Read 3: Comprehension

- Ask the children if they like the dark winter evenings, and why or why not.
- Discuss the title. Ask: Do you think the title fits the theme of the story? Why?
- Discuss Fred's feelings and what cheers him up.
  - Reread pages 2 and 3. Ask: How is Fred feeling and why? (e.g. *it's winter and the dark evenings stop Fred from playing outside*)
  - Reread page 5 and ask: How does Dad try to cheer up Fred? (e.g. *he shows how it can be fun to play with a torch and have hot drinks*) Ask: What cheers up Fred in the end? (*visiting a fair and seeing a firework display*)
  - Ask the children what they would do to cheer up a friend who felt glum.
- Look at pages 14 and 15. Encourage the children to use the pictures to help them retell the story in the correct sequence. Talk about how Fred feels in each picture.